FINDING PRINT & SUBSCRIPTION SOURCES

VALERIE BODDEN | ILLUSTRATIONS BY ELWOOD H. SMITH

CREATIVE ❦ EDUCATION

Published by Creative Education
P.O. Box 227, Mankato, Minnesota 56002
Creative Education is an imprint of The Creative Company
www.thecreativecompany.us

Design and production by Liddy Walseth
Art direction by Rita Marshall
Printed in the United States of America

Illustrations by Elwood H. Smith © 2012

Library of Congress Cataloging-in-Publication Data

Bodden, Valerie.
Finding print and subscription sources / by Valerie Bodden.
p. cm. — (Research for writing)
Includes bibliographical references and index.
Summary: A narrative guide to conducting research with print and
subscription sources, complete with an overview of methodologies,
tips for locating reference works and periodicals, and helpful resources.
ISBN 978-1-60818-205-3
1. Research—Methodology—Juvenile literature. 2. Reference books—Juvenile
literature. 3. Periodicals—Databases—Juvenile literature. 4. Library
research—Juvenile literature. 5. Information literacy—Juvenile literature. I. Title.

ZA3080.B635 2012
001.4'2—dc23   2011040491

First Edition
2 4 6 8 9 7 5 3 1

TABLE OF CONTENTS

YOU CONDUCT RESEARCH EVERY DAY.
AND YOU PROBABLY DON'T EVEN REALIZE IT.

When you want to know the score of last night's football game, you check online. If you're wondering how to spell (or define) "supercilious," you get out the dictionary. And when you've forgotten the math assignment, you e-mail your friends to ask them. Although these research situations are rather informal, the skills you use for them are similar to those you need to conduct research for writing. After all, research is basically just a search—a search for sources that contain specific, **relevant**, and accurate information about your topic.

At the heart of nearly any research assignment are print sources—books, newspapers, journals, magazines, and more. Why? These sources can provide useful background information as well as in-depth coverage of almost any topic imaginable—from Antarctica to zebras. Let's say, for example, that you have been asked to write about air pollution. You can start the writing process by going to the library and checking out several books, downloading online journal articles, and even viewing government records on the Internet.

With the hundreds of thousands of new books published every year, along with millions of articles, how do you even begin to find the ones you need? Fortunately, library catalogs and **databases** categorize print resources according to their subjects, authors, titles, and more. And hundreds of reference books provide additional information on general subjects, along with lists of where to get more. With so many resources at your fingertips, it will be hard not to find something about your topic!

LEARNING HOW TO LEARN

YOU ARE SURROUNDED BY PRINT RESOURCES. At home, at school, even at the doctor's office, you will find books, magazines, and newspapers, among others. In fact, you probably already have favorite books and magazines— and those books and magazines might even be useful for some of your research. If your favorite book is Madeleine L'Engle's *A Wrinkle in Time*, for example, you could use it as a source for a paper about the author or about science fantasy literature. Or, if your favorite magazine is *Sports Illustrated*, it might serve as a source for a writing assignment on a specific sports star, the use of steroids in professional sports, or sports history. Chances are, though, that you'll need to search farther afield than what you can find at home for information on many topics.

Before you can begin that search, you need to know what you are looking for, where to find it, and how to evaluate it. These key skills are known as information literacy, and according to the American Library Association, a person who has mastered them has "learned how to learn." The first step in the process of becoming information literate—and in doing any research, with print sources or otherwise—is to determine what kind of information you need. That might seem obvious, but it takes some planning. If, for example, your topic is Africa, you are going to be overwhelmed if you simply search for books and articles about the continent. The world's largest library, the Library of Congress in Washington, D.C., for example, lists more than 10,000 books relating to Africa in its catalog. That's a bit too much reading for anyone—it would take hours just to read through the list of titles! Even your local public library may have close to 1,000 items on the subject. When you find this many results about a single subject, it's a clue that your topic is too broad; you need to narrow it. Perhaps there is a certain country or a theme about Africa (wildlife or famine, for example) that interests you. Or maybe you have no idea what it is that you want to write about Africa. That's okay, too. Do some background reading in a resource such as an encyclopedia—you may just find your interest piqued by some specific aspect of the topic.

After some careful thought and background research, perhaps you have narrowed your topic to elementary schools in Africa. Now that you know your topic, another step in the process of becoming information literate is identifying the keywords that you can use to search for information about it. Although you could try simply searching for "elementary schools in Africa," you may end up with few or no relevant results. This does not mean that nothing has been written on the topic; it may be that you haven't yet found the right words to discover what has been

IDENTIFYING THE KEYWORDS

written. As you think about potential keywords, consider **synonyms** as well as related terms. Instead of "elementary," for example, you might search for "primary" (another word often used to refer to the early years of school) or "grade school." And in place of "schools," you could try "education." You might even search for "literacy" or "attendance," since these are some subjects that may be found in works related to education. Once you find a good source, reading through it may give you ideas for additional search terms as well. Make a list of all your keywords and use it to aid in your search, noting which words yield the best results—that way you won't have to try all of your keywords every time you want to look for a new source.

Once you've identified your keywords, you can take the next step in becoming information literate—go out and find your sources. And then you're done with your research, right? Not quite. Before you use those sources, you need to evaluate them to decide whether the information they contain is credible. Whether you are looking at a book or an article, consider the author. Is she a recognized expert on the subject? Many works provide a short **biography** listing the author's credentials, but you can also search for information about the author on the Internet. For general interest magazine and newspaper articles, the author is often a journalist rather than a recognized scholar on a particular topic, but you can still check her publishing credits. You can also consider the organization that published the information. Academic presses, such as Harvard University Press, are often trustworthy. These presses, along with academic journals, often print only works that have been reviewed and approved by a panel of peers, or experts in the field. Newspaper and magazine articles do not go through such a rigorous examination before being printed, but if they appear in a reputable source such as *The New York Times*, they are generally reliable.

Another way to check the accuracy of a source is to verify that its author has provided adequate documentation. If there is a **bibliography**, dig into some of the sources listed. Do they say what the author claims they say? Are they reputable? Don't be afraid to compare one source's information with another's. Reference works such as encyclopedias and dictionaries are usually reliable and can be used to check facts or statistics **cited** in another work. Also consider when the work was published. For some

CHECK FACTS OR STATISTICS CITED

subjects, such as history or literature, an older work may still provide usable information, but for others, especially in science or technology, only the most up-to-date information will do.

Even if a source is authoritative and current, it may still be **biased**. Compare the views expressed in one source with those in another. Does one source seem to support a specific viewpoint or interpretation? Consider the author's background or purpose. For example, an author who is a vegetarian may provide data in her article supporting the health benefits of a diet rich in fruits and vegetables but may neglect to add any information about the health benefits of eating meat. Bias is not necessarily wrong (in fact, we all have certain biases), but you need to be aware of it so that you can interpret an author's viewpoint.

Finally, as you search for sources, you need to determine whether they are relevant to your topic. No matter how accurate the information you find is, it won't do you any good if it doesn't relate to your topic. If you are researching ancient Greek sculpture for example, works about Greek paintings are not likely to provide useful information (unless you want to compare them with Greek sculpture). You can skim a book's introduction or glance through its **index** to determine if it will be helpful. For articles, browse the beginnings of each section or read an abstract, or summary, of the work to help you decide whether or not to use it. As you do so, you might also pay attention to the language of the source. If it is too difficult to comprehend, then it probably won't be much help in your research. After all, it's hard to describe to others what you can't understand yourself.

PUT THEM IN QUOTATION MARKS

Once you've found and evaluated your sources, be sure to use them correctly. Keep track of each source's author, title, publisher, and publication date, and if you use an idea that isn't your own, be sure to cite where it came from. Likewise, if you use someone else's words directly, put them in quotation marks. Once you've figured out what you need and how to obtain, evaluate, and cite it, you'll be on the road to information literacy—and a great research project!

EXPLORING EVALUATION

Learning to evaluate sources takes practice. First, choose a nonfiction book about any subject that interests you. Before you even begin to read it, take a look at its author. Does the book provide a biography listing her credentials (this can often be found inside the back cover)? Do a search for the author online. Does it appear that she is a recognized expert in the field? Check the book's publication information, too. Who is the publisher—is it an academic press (such as a university)? When was the book published—is it current? Does the date matter for the subject? Scan the introduction and the first paragraphs of a few chapters. Does the book appear to be well written? Can you understand the language? Are the subjects covered relevant to your topic? When you are done, draw some conclusions about whether the book would make a good source for your research.

HITTING
THE BOOKS
(AND ARTICLES)

PRINT SOURCES ARE OFTEN CATEGORIZED AS BEING EITHER PRIMARY OR SECONDARY. But what does that mean? Are primary sources the best sources or the first sources you should consult? Not necessarily. "Primary" simply refers to the fact that a source contains direct, firsthand information from an eyewitness observer. Nothing stands between the original source and the event or information it relates. A newspaper account of an event is a primary source. So are **autobiographies**, letters, diary entries, speeches, interviews, and novels. Even maps, government documents such as reports or proceedings, and photographs serve as primary sources, as do articles publishing the results of original research.

Secondary sources, on the other hand, report on—and often interpret—primary sources. They rely on the information-gathering and analysis of a secondary author—someone who was not present for an event. Secondary sources include encyclopedias, biographies, and other books or articles that interpret an earlier event or an earlier researcher's findings. For example, if you are researching Abraham Lincoln, then his famous speech called the Gettysburg Address would be a primary source, while an encyclopedia entry or a biography of the president would be a secondary source. Because of their firsthand nature, primary sources are great for conveying the emotional impact of an event—but they can also contain inaccuracies or bias. A soldier on one side of a war is going to see events differently from a soldier on the other side, for example. Secondary sources, while perhaps lacking some of that emotional impact, may also be more **objective**.

Both primary and secondary sources are valuable in the research process. In fact, you will often want to begin your research with secondary sources. Why? Secondary sources provide background information, which can help you to better understand your primary sources and their significance. Secondary sources can also lead you to primary sources. For example, if you are researching the Declaration of Independence, you might start by reading an encyclopedia article. From that article, you might learn that, although Thomas Jefferson drafted the document, the Continental Congress made a number of changes before adopting it. Perhaps this will lead you to

search for a copy of Jefferson's original draft—which you will now be able to better understand, thanks to your prior knowledge of the document.

In addition to progressing from secondary sources to primary sources, you will also typically want to work your way from the general to the more specific. The most generalized sources are reference works such as encyclopedias and dictionaries. These provide only a brief overview of a topic. While a book on the Vietnam War might be 700-plus pages long, for example, an encyclopedia might cover the same topic in 10 to 20 pages, and a dictionary could summarize the war in fewer than 50 words. Nearly every library has a large collection of encyclopedias, dictionaries, and other reference works, and a growing number of reference materials are available online as well.

Providing slightly more specific information than encyclopedias—though still not an in-depth treatment of a subject—general interest magazines (such as *Time*, *Redbook*, and *Sports Illustrated*) and newspapers provide useful information on a number of topics, particularly current events and popular culture. During a political election, for example, magazines and newspapers cover candidates' speeches, views, and personal backgrounds well before books or reference works can be printed with such details. Current newspapers and magazines can be found in the library's periodicals section. Articles from older issues of major national newspapers such as *The New York Times* or of hometown papers may be stored on microfilm (or microfiche)—a film format that can be read only by a special machine in the library. Today, most libraries also have online databases providing summaries or full-text articles from both newspapers and magazines. In addition, several sources, such as *The New York Times* and *Time* magazine, have searchable

archives on their Web sites, although a fee is sometimes required to view the full text of articles.

If you are ready for a more in-depth treatment of your topic, you will likely find it in a book, unless your topic is so recent or involves such new developments that books about it have not yet been published. Many books on current technology, for example, are outdated before they even hit the shelves. As you look for books, be sure to consider both primary and secondary sources. If you are looking for information on

LIBRARIES ALSO HAVE ONLINE DATABASES

the 1945 bombing of Hiroshima, Japan, for example, you might search for books by survivors of the bombing, as well as titles that provide secondary interpretations of the lasting effects of the event. Secondary sources also often provide excerpts from primary sources and can lead you to further resources through notes and bibliographies.

Books can, of course, be found in libraries and bookstores, but a growing selection of books is also available online. Sites such as Project Gutenberg (www.gutenberg.org) and Bartleby.com (www.bartleby.com) provide e-books that can be read online or downloaded for free. In general, these books were published before about 1920 and are now in the public domain (which means that their **copyright** has expired). One advantage of e-books is that they can be easily searched (using your Internet browser's search tool) to find specific words or phrases.

When you need the latest scholarship on a subject, journal articles are the place to turn. Although they look much like general interest magazines, journals are usually intended for a specific, expert audience. So, while you may find a short article about school lunches in a general interest magazine such as *Time*, you could find a more in-depth

ARCHITECTURE TO DANCE

treatment of the subject, including detailed study results, tables, and charts comparing childhood **obesity** rates and participation in school lunch programs in a publication such as the *Journal of School Health*. Because they are intended for an expert audience, journal articles can make for difficult reading. That is one of the reasons that you will consult them toward the end of your research process—by now you will have an idea of the terms and concepts used in works on your subject. Keep in mind, though, that there may be some journal articles that you simply can't use because of the level of expertise required to read them.

You can find journals on nearly every subject, from architecture to dance, calculus to kidneys. Your library probably subscribes to at least some journals in print and has access to numerous more through an online database. Although most journals charge a subscription fee (which is why it can be best to access them through your library's database), some are also available for free online. You can search for them on Web sites such as JURN (www.jurn.org) or the Directory of Open Access Journals (www.doaj.org).

If your research has to do with laws or public policy, you may find some aspects of the topic covered in journal articles. But you might also consider searching government and legal documents. Court rulings or opinions for some cases are available through local courthouses (and a number of states also make this information available online). In addition, your library may have some governmental records, especially those pertaining to local government. In the United States, a number of university and larger public libraries in each state have been designated as

CALCULUS TO KIDNEYS

Federal Depository Libraries, which means they house copies of federally published documents. For more in-depth research, the National Archives and Records Administration operates a number of archives throughout the country (in locations such as Atlanta, Georgia; Chicago, Illinois; and Seattle, Washington) that hold public records about the nation's history and people. Some of these records can also be found on the organization's Web site (www.archives.gov). So hit the books (and magazines, newspapers, journals, and Web sites), and you'll be an authority on your topic in no time!

PUTTING IT IN PRINT

Printed sources have been used to record and communicate information for thousands of years. The earliest "books" date from around 3000 B.C. Unlike the paper-and-ink form we know today, however, the first books were made on tablets of clay in Mesopotamia and rolls of papyrus (a paper-like writing material made from the papyrus plant) in Egypt. Around 1300 B.C., the Chinese began creating books of wood or bamboo strips. By about the 4th century A.D., books in Rome were appearing in codex form on parchment (dried animal skins). It was not until about the 15th century A.D. that paper was used regularly for books. Until then, the only way to produce books was to copy them by hand. The invention of the printing press in Germany around 1450 changed all that, bringing about an explosion in book publishing. Book production has only continued to grow in the years since. Today, more than one million books are published worldwide every year.

READ YOUR REFERENCES

SO YOU WANT TO BEGIN YOUR SEARCH WITH SECONDARY SOURCES

providing general information—in other words, reference works. But are all reference materials the same? How do you find the ones you need? And how do you even use them?

In short, a reference work is a work in which information about several topics has been gathered, sorted, and summarized. The kind of reference work you need depends on the information for which you're looking. Some reference works, such as encyclopedias, almanacs, and fact books, provide general information about a topic; others, such as bibliographies and indexes, provide lists of sources where you can find more information. For example, if you are researching horror literature, you might look for an article summarizing the subject in an encyclopedia; then, if you want to know more about works by specific horror authors, you might look through the entries in a bibliographic index.

In general, libraries provide both kinds of reference works in their reference section. Books shelved here are usually non-circulating—they must be used in the library. You can find them by browsing the shelves or by searching your library's catalog. Some reference works may also be available through your library's online databases or on the Internet. Once you find the reference work you need, the idea is not to read it through from start to finish. Some of these works may run to 30 or more

volumes—and that could take years to read! Instead, look for the entry (or entries) pertaining to your topic and gather what you need from that. Most reference works are arranged alphabetically, topically, or chronologically (by date). And if you aren't sure where to find your subject, you can always check the index, which is often printed in a separate volume.

Often, the best place to turn for an initial overview of your subject is an encyclopedia. That sounds simple enough. But when you reach your library's

ENCYCLOPEDIAS ALMANACS BIOGRAPHICAL DICTIONARIES

reference section, you will soon realize that there are all kinds of encyclopedias— and not all will be useful in finding information on your topic. Encyclopedias can be divided into two broad categories: general and specialized. General encyclopedias provide short articles on a wide variety of subjects. Among the best-known are *Encyclopaedia Britannica*, *Grolier*, and *World Book*. These works can give you an overview of your topic and introduce you to its key terminology. In addition, the bibliographies provided at the end of the article can give you a starting point for finding further resources. Many general encyclopedias can also be found online (although most charge a fee or are available only through a library subscription) and offer additional features beyond the print versions of the works, such as links to related articles and audiovisual materials, as well as frequent article updates. You can find your topic by searching the site or by browsing a list of subjects.

Specialized encyclopedias can be harder to find online, but a trip to the library to use them is often well worth it. These works focus on a single field, such as art or religion, and provide in-depth articles on different aspects of that field. If, for example, you are researching Dutch painter Vincent van Gogh, you might check the *Encyclopedia of World Art*, *The Macmillan Encyclopedia of Art*, or *The Oxford Dictionary of Art* (similar to an encyclopedia but with briefer entries). Other types of specialized reference works include biographical dictionaries, which provide entries on famous or noted people. A biographical dictionary may focus on a certain time period, nation, or field in its selection of subjects.

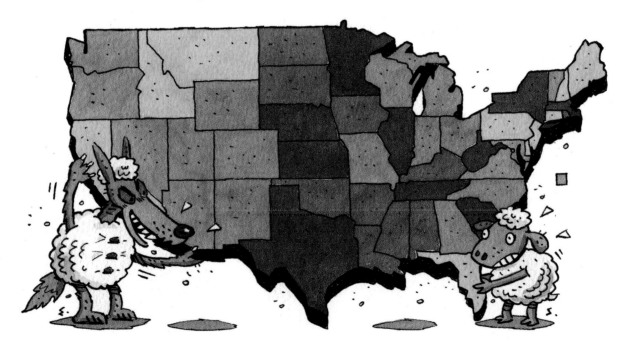

Encyclopedias are not the only types of reference works you can turn to for information, though. If you need cold, hard facts—dates, numbers, or names—you can check fact books such as almanacs and statistical yearbooks. Almanacs, which are usually published annually, contain a wide, somewhat eclectic collection of facts, often including timelines of the year's biggest events, population statistics, and sports records. As their name suggests, statistical yearbooks focus on statistics, providing figures and tables relating to topics such as population, immigration, and religion. So, if you want to know what percentage of people in Pakistan are Muslim, Christian, or Hindu, you could consult a statistical yearbook. Although most almanacs and statistical yearbooks can be found in print, some are available online as well, such as *The World Factbook* (https://www.cia.gov/library/publications/the-world-factbook/index.html), which contains information on the world's countries and people, as compiled by the U.S. Central Intelligence Agency.

While encyclopedias and fact books provide you with information about your topic right there on their pages, some reference works are designed to guide you to information printed in other sources. Usually referred to as bibliographies or indexes (or sometimes as bibliographic indexes), these works provide listings of books or articles relevant to a specific subject—such as *The Music Index* or the *Bibliography and Index of Geology*. Bibliographies include the publication information you need (author, title, publisher, date, etc.) to help you locate the works listed. Unlike a library catalog, though, bibliographies do not provide you with a **call number** to locate the material (nor do they even tell you if your library owns a copy). Instead, they simply provide you with a list of the scholarship available on your topic. Some bibliographies are also annotated—meaning they contain notes or summaries of the works listed—which can help you decide whether a specific book or article might be useful for your research. Unfortunately, the lag time between when a book or article appears in print and when it is added to a bibliography can be long, meaning that bibliographies may not contain the most up-to-date resources. In addition to print bibliographies, your library may also provide access to these sources through its online database.

Of course, the reference section of your library is not the only place to find books on your subject. Chances are, your library's collection of circulating nonfiction titles is much larger than its reference collection. In fact, there are so many books that it's hard to know where to begin your search. You could wander the stacks aimlessly for days and still not find anything you need. Fortunately, libraries do not toss their books randomly onto the shelves. Instead, they arrange them by subject matter and then catalog them. That way, you can search the catalog, find out where the books you need are located, and retrieve them.

Today, most libraries use online catalogs, which you can search by keyword, subject, author, or title. If you have consulted the bibliographies of encyclopedia articles or searched through a bibliographic index, you might know exactly what books you are looking for, so you can search for them by entering the author's name or the title of the work. If, on the other hand, you aren't sure exactly what you are looking for, you can search by subject or keyword. This is where your list of keywords generated even before you started researching might come in handy.

Once you have discovered a book that looks relevant, remember that you don't have to read the whole thing (although you can, if you'd like). Instead, check the index for pages containing information relevant to your topic. If, for

HANDS ON SOME BOOKS

example, you are researching Michelle Obama in a book about U.S. president Barack Obama, you may want to skip over the portions about the president's childhood and instead focus on when he met his future wife. And, of course, if you want to be able to use your source outside the library, be sure to get a library card so that you can check it out. Once you get your hands on some books, it should be easy to learn the ins and outs of your topic!

TOURING THE REFERENCE SECTION

The reference section of your library may seem like a formidable place. After all, it is filled with row upon row of thick, academic-looking books. But once you get to know what's there, you'll find that navigating the reference section is no trouble—and well worth the effort. First, pick a broad topic (maybe outer space) and look for a general encyclopedia article on it. Skim the article and note any narrower topics that interest you (maybe space travel, for example). Now, try to find a specialized encyclopedia on your topic. You can do so by browsing the shelves or searching your library's catalog (using terms such as "space travel encyclopedia," perhaps). After you've looked for a specialized encyclopedia, try to find a bibliographic index for your topic. Glance through it to see how many books pertain to your subject. If you wanted to research this topic in-depth, would there be enough information available? Or would there be too much?

ARTICLES
WITH
ANSWERS

MOST BOOKS ARE PRINTED ONLY ONCE. Or they might be printed once and then later updated and reprinted. Newspapers, magazines, and journals, on the other hand, are printed much more frequently—quarterly, monthly, weekly, or even daily—and each issue contains new content. In addition, while most traditional books are written by one or a few authors, periodicals contain a number of articles written by several different authors. While the titles of the articles in a periodical differ from one issue to the next, the periodical itself is always published under the same name and prints works in the same subject area—news, for example, or history or women's issues. Most periodicals are distributed by subscription. That is, for an annual fee, you will receive all the issues of the periodical published during the year. Your family may even have one or two subscriptions—maybe to the local newspaper or a cooking magazine. Libraries also maintain subscriptions to a number of periodicals—both in print and through online databases. Some periodicals also provide their contents on their Web sites, although you may need a subscription to view the full content.

If your topic pertains to a local issue or current events, your best source might be newspaper articles. For example, if you want to write about the debate over whether to build a new library in your city, your hometown paper will probably be the best (and perhaps the only) source for printed information on the topic. Newspapers can also provide specific examples to illustrate a point. For a paper on speed limits, for example, you might consult newspaper accounts of a car accident in which the victims were speeding.

Although print indexes such as *The New York Times Index* were once the main way of locating newspaper articles, most libraries today rely on online newspaper indexes, some of which provide abstracts or even the full text of articles. Some of the more common newspaper databases found in libraries include National Newspaper Index, Proquest National Newspapers, and Newspaper Source. Most of these sources index only the largest national and regional newspapers, so if you are looking for information about your hometown, you could check the local newspaper's Web site or ask your **reference librarian** where to find an index of back issues.

The articles in magazines and journals are generally longer than those in newspapers. In addition, while newspaper articles usually stick to the facts—who, what, where, when, and how—magazine and journal articles may go beyond the facts and enter the realm of interpretation. You already

know that magazines are usually aimed at a general audience, while journals are intended for experts in the subject. But how, really, can you tell the difference? If you see a magazine and a journal next to each other on the racks at the library, how will you know which is which? To begin with, their covers can give you a clue: general magazines are usually glossy and colorful, with a snappy title (such as *Wired*), while journals may look more formal, with a straightforward, informative title (such as *Computer Protocols*). Still, you may not always be able to tell by the cover. In that case, flip the periodical open. Magazines will likely be filled with colorful pictures and advertisements, and the writing style of articles—which are mostly written by journalists rather than experts in the field—will probably be rather casual (although this does not mean that magazines do not cover serious topics). Journals, on the other hand, may have charts and graphs but will probably have fewer photos or ads, and their articles—by experts in the field—will be written in formal, academic language, often peppered with the field's **jargon**. Most articles will probably also

WHO WHAT WHERE WHEN HOW

 have **footnotes** and bibliographies. One other minor characteristic that might help you spot the difference between the two types of periodicals is that each issue of a magazine is generally paginated, or given page numbers, separately, while journals may have continuous pagination (so that if the summer issue ends at page 105, the fall issue begins with page 106, for example). Ultimately, your periodical search will most likely involve both types of articles, as you start by reading the more generalized magazine accounts and then move on to the specifics provided by journals.

Knowing the difference between magazines and journals won't do you much good, though, if you don't know how to find the articles you need inside. In the reference section of many libraries, you will find a book called *Readers' Guide to Periodical Literature*. This multi-volume index provides bibliographic information for the articles published in more than 300 periodicals, with a new volume released each month. Each volume is arranged alphabetically by subject and author. So if you are looking for current articles written about horse racing, you would go to the most recent volume of *Readers' Guide* and look under the subject "horse racing." At the end of the year, all the volumes from January to December are compiled into one book. In addition to *Readers' Guide*, which provides information on a wide range of fields, there are specialized periodical indexes that list works printed in journals and magazines related to a specific discipline, such as art or education. Your library may also have abstract collections, which provide summaries in addition to bibliographic information about articles.

While *Readers' Guide* and similar print indexes were once the only way to search for magazine and journal articles, today most libraries subscribe to online periodical databases (and in some libraries, these have completely replaced print indexes). *Readers' Guide*, for example, is available online. Other periodical databases to which your library might subscribe include EBSCO Academic Search Premier, LexisNexis Academic, and JSTOR. You can generally find links to these databases on your library's Web site (and

you may even be able to access them from a computer outside the library by entering your library card number). Searching online databases is even easier than flipping open a book. Just enter your terms (here are those keywords again) in the search field—and voilà!—you'll see results. Many databases also provide a way to search a specific publication, issue date, or article or author name. If you've mined the bibliography of another article, for example, you might know exactly what you are looking for—and you'll be able to find it easily.

Once you have hit upon an article that looks promising, you might discover that the full text is available through the database. If so, great! If not, don't despair. Make note of the bibliographical information and check if your library subscribes to a print version of the magazine or journal. Even if it doesn't, you may still be able to get a copy of it through **interlibrary loan**—just see

MIGHT BE ABLE TO TEACH YOUR READERS

your reference librarian for details on how to make a request. Although the information for many of the titles indexed in databases is updated frequently—and some provide almost up-to-the-minute updates—this is not the case for all items. For this reason, you might want to take a walk through your library's current periodicals section. A quick glance through the tables of contents of any magazines or journals that might be relevant to your topic might just net you an article that you wouldn't have found otherwise.

From journals, magazines, and newspapers to books and reference works, print resources are a mainstay of performing research on nearly any topic. Learning when to use them, where to find them, and how to search for them will help to make you an effective researcher. So start gathering—and reading—printed words. You'd be surprised what you might learn—and what you might be able to teach your readers!

ADVANCING YOUR SEARCH

As you search a periodical database, you may find that you come up with too many results (in which case your search is too broad) or too few (in which case your search is too narrow or you haven't hit on the right keyword). Either way, you need to refine your search. You can do this by creating a Boolean search using the words "and," "or," and "not." For example, maybe you are searching for information on oil drilling in areas of the U.S. other than Alaska. In that case, you might enter into the search box "oil drilling and U.S. not Alaska." Most databases also have an advanced search function to help you create a Boolean search, often with boxes labeled "include all these terms" or "include none of these terms." The advanced search screen is also where you can enter a specific publication name or date to search.

GLOSSARY

archives—collections of documents or items of historical importance, or the buildings (or online locations) where such documents or items are stored

autobiographies—stories of a person's life, written by the person him- or herself

biased—having a preference for or dislike of a certain person or idea that prevents one from making impartial judgments of that person or idea

bibliography—a list of books used in the preparation of a book or article or of books on a specific subject or by a specific author, along with publication information (author, title, publisher, date) for each

biography—the history of a person's life, written by someone other than that person

Boolean—a system of logic that combines the words "and," "or," and "not" to establish relationships between terms and ideas

call number—a series of numbers and letters assigned to a book to indicate its position on a library's shelves

cited—quoted someone else's work as evidence for an idea or argument

codex—the earliest form of modern books, with separate pages bound together along one edge

copyright—the legal right of an author or artist to exclusively publish or reproduce his or her works

databases—organized collections of data, or information, stored on a computer

footnotes—notes printed at the bottom of a page to provide additional information or references about a specific point in the text

index—in the context of books and articles, a catalog or list of specific items, often arranged alphabetically and providing details about where to find them

interlibrary loan—a system that involves borrowing a book from another library without visiting that library in person

jargon—special words used by people within a specific profession or field that are typically not understood by others outside the field

Mesopotamia—a region in present-day Iraq and Syria that was home to several ancient civilizations, such as the Babylonians

obesity—a condition in which a person is dangerously overweight

objective—unbiased and based on facts rather than feelings

reference librarian—a professional trained to find and organize information in a library and elsewhere

relevant—related or connected to the idea or topic being discussed

synonyms—words that have the same (or nearly the same) meaning

WEB SITES

Encyclopedia.com

http://www.encyclopedia.com/

Access the online versions of encyclopedias and other reference works.

Evaluating Sources of Information

http://owl.english.purdue.edu/owl/resource/553/01/

Review the steps every researcher should take to evaluate his or her sources and citations.

Research Minutes: How to Identify Scholarly Journal Articles

http://www.youtube.com/watch?v=uDGJ2CYfY9A

Watch this short video about how to recognize and find journal articles in a library.

What Are Primary Sources?

http://www.yale.edu/collections_collaborative/primarysources/primarysources.html

Find out more about different types of primary documents.

SELECTED BIBLIOGRAPHY

Anson, Chris M., Robert A. Schwegler, and Marcia F. Muth. *The Longman Writer's Bible: The Complete Guide to Writing, Research, and Grammar*. New York: Pearson Longman, 2006.

Ballenger, Bruce. *The Curious Researcher: A Guide to Writing Research Papers*. New York: Pearson Longman, 2004.

Booth, Wayne C., Gregory G. Colomb, and Joseph M. Williams. *The Craft of Research*. Chicago: University of Chicago Press, 2008.

George, Mary W. *The Elements of Library Research: What Every Student Needs to Know*. Princeton: Princeton University Press, 2008.

Lane, Nancy, Margaret Chisholm, and Carolyn Mateer. *Techniques for Student Research: A Comprehensive Guide to Using the Library*. New York: Neal-Schuman Publishers, 2000.

MLA Handbook for Writers of Research Papers. New York: The Modern Language Association of America, 2009.

Rodrigues, Dawn, and Raymond J. Rodrigues. *The Research Paper: A Guide to Library and Internet Research*. Upper Saddle River, N.J.: Prentice Hall, 2003.

Toronto Public Library. *The Research Virtuoso: Brilliant Methods for Normal Brains*. Toronto: Annick Press, 2006.

INDEX